# Knowle

# Acceptance,

# Compassion

A journey of learning about, understanding, and
responding to people as individuals

# By Denise Ghizzone

# Table of Contents

# Introduction

Many people who didn't know me prior to reading my first book said I am good at expressing myself and making people really think about what I am saying. They keep asking me if I'm going to write a book called "Determination: What I'm All About, continuation!"

Then I started to think about doing that very thing. You are holding the proof that I decided to do it! This time I am going to educate other people on how to treat people with disabilities. People with disabilities are the same as everybody in this world! We're human beings, whether we look different, are sitting in a wheelchair, or are using a communication device. Many people see the outside and worry about catching something from people that are different. What about talking to a disabled person, getting to know the inside of them and not paying attention to what is on the outside?

In order to do this, it helps to think about the ways in which we are all alike. For example, as we get older, most of us have to start to change in our daily routines. For example, oftentimes people start wearing glasses, taking medicine, or eating healthy to counteract physical symptoms. That is a fact of life, no matter if you are disabled or not. There was a time of my life I was facing some physical issues. In the back of my mind I knew that I had to accept that my body would give out eventually. Everything must come to an end some time, but that thought didn't hold me down. So, I may have had to deal with some of these issues earlier and more often than some others, but it's a part of life that we all share.

I had some bad experiences with doctors and nurses in the hospital and rehab units. I thought they would have better bedside matters for people with disabilities; after all, they work in the health field! But I was wrong. They didn't treat me very nicely and they weren't very accommodating to me.

My parents never protected me from life. A couple of times my dad was taken to the hospital by an ambulance. Each time my mom explained to me that he had to go to the hospital because he was very sick, but he would be okay. I knew everybody gets sick now and then. It's part of life!

My parents taught me about death and not to be scared about it. When I was younger my grandmother and aunt died. I went to their funerals. I was scared, but I had my mom, dad, and brother there. It was okay. I was never raised in a plastic bubble, and they were honest with me. But there was one very important thing they forgot to tell me: they never told me what I would do without them when they died! I think I know by now because I am still here. I made some mistakes along the way. I never regret those mistakes. That's what everybody does -- that's life!

I lost my mom in 1998. She went in her sleep all of a sudden. That was hard for me, but I managed. In 2000, my dad got sick and died. In a later chapter, I will share about his death and about some fun times with him when I was younger! Without those two people in my life, life became hard for me. I know my parents didn't want me to be unhappy for the rest of my life. I wasn't raised like that, so I pushed ahead in life. They are with me forever in my heart!

In this book I will give you some things to think about people with disabilities. People often think differently on this subject. I am disabled, and I can tell how other people perceive me just by talking to me. This is especially true about employers, doctors, and nurses, but also includes other people.

After my graduation, I was looking for a job for years. I found some employers to be narrow minded. I feel they should give people with disabilities a real chance at a job. After my firsthand experiences with employers and doctors and how they treated me, I came to the conclusion that they don't understand people with disabilities: who they are and how to help them.

I am 50 years old and I still have some experiences with all kind of attitudes from people. By now, I am very used to those bad attitudes. You might be one who doesn't understand what people with disabilities must go through each day. I'm going to give you the benefit of the doubt and trust you want to understand, so I'll try to help you by means of this book. Oftentimes people haven't a clue how to interact with people with disabilities. It's a shame because we are incredible people. I sometimes surprise myself with the things I can do!

I am a teacher and a motivational speaker, and I am very good at reading how other people react towards me. There are some people that just look at my power chair and communication device. They seem to overlook the intelligent and educated person driving the power chair and using the communication device. Power chairs and communication devices are very difficult to work, so simply being able to operate them demonstrates that the person is smart and worth getting to know about in terms of interests, goals, and so forth. There are various reasons people with disabilities should get specialized equipment. This equipment will help them to be more independent. Therefore, people with disabilities want to be independent for themselves. They need a power chair, communication device or something else to achieve their goals. People with disabilities want to be like everybody else! They have to have a lot of patience and talent to operate power chairs and communication devices.

The last thing I will share with you in this book are some of my short stories. I am proud of being an Author because I did it myself, with some help along the way. I have trouble with my grammar and spelling, but that doesn't stop me from writing.

Writing puts me into another world. When I write, I can be anybody I want, and say anything I want without people knowing if I am disabled or not.

I am dedicating this book to all my teachers and speech therapists over the years at Ladacin Network. I thank them for teaching me how to read and spell and getting me communication devices.

My parents were the first and most important influence and support in my life. But right behind them were all my instructors and tutors at Brookdale community college. For all your hard work with me, I thank you too. I hope you agree that all your dedication towards me paid off.

## My dad!

After my mom passed, my dad lived alone in our house in Atlantic Highlands for the last two years of his life. He was doing well there for two years, but then he went downhill. My brother was living with my dad during that time period.

I'll never forget the day my brother called me to say that our dad was in the hospital. He was in and out of the hospital all that summer. Every part of his body was giving out on him. He was not doing well at all. When I went to visit him, I had some flashbacks of him when I was growing up in our house. Let me describe them to you.

*First flashback*: Thanksgiving: my mom always cooked our Thanksgiving dinner. We used to have mashed potatoes, peas and carrots, cranberry sauce, turnips, biscuits, turkey, gravy, and of course my favorite: homemade stuffing. She would cook all day. I was on the couch in the living room, smelling all the great cooking in the kitchen. Nobody cooked like my mom!

When the turkey was done, my dad used to sneak me some stuffing from the kitchen. He would go on his tippy toes, very quietly put the stuffing in my mouth, and sit down in his rocking chair fast before my mom would catch him.

Wherever my mom came from, she would ask me, did Dad give you some stuffing? I just shook my head no with a big smile on my face! She knew he did. My dad would say I gave it away with my smile!

*Second flashback*: When my brother and I were younger, my dad used to put up our Christmas tree lights and decorations on our house. My dad would go up in the attic to get the Christmas tree and decorations. He loved to put the Christmas lights on the tree. Not really; in fact, he didn't like that job because the lights got all tangled up. He sat on the floor to untangle them. Even though he didn't like the job, he was good at it. He got frustrated a lot, but eventually he got them on the tree. Every year I watched him on the couch doing the lights. I didn't like to watch him because I could hear him cursing under his breath.

He also brought down a long plastic Santa's sled and eight reindeers. My dad always put it on the roof with nails, wood, and rope to attach Santa and his eight reindeers! After my dad was done, my mom would carry me in her arms outside to see the Christmas decorations when it was dark.

*Third flashback*: My dad used to tell me that when I was 4 or 5 years old, he would take my brother and me for a sleigh ride. He attached my wooden chair on the sled with ropes. We used to live at the bottom of a hill. When it snowed, everything was covered in white. My dad took us to the top of the hill for a sleigh ride. He let us go down the hill fast. Yes, my dad put a strap around me, so I would stay in. My mom was never there to watch us. She didn't want to see me get hurt in any way. She was very protective of me in those situations. She was being a good mom. On the other hand my dad would let me try anything when I was with him. I learned how not to be afraid of anything from my dad. He was right there beside me when he was doing these things.

*Fourth flashback*: When I was younger, my dad bought a series of above-ground pools throughout my childhood and some of my teenage years. My favorite thing to do with my dad in the pool was when I was in an inner tube, and he would pick me up in the tube. We used to live on Second Avenue, and the back of our house faced First Avenue. He would say "See First Avenue?" By this time, I would be laughing and say Yes over his head. I would hold my breath because I knew what was coming next! He would throw me up in the air and let me fall into the water fast. I made a big splash in the water when I came down. I got a big kick out of that. Of course, my mom would stay in the house for all this, so she wouldn't have to see if I got hurt.

*Fifth flashback*: My dad's driving was memorable to me. My dad had to drive my mom and me to the hospital a lot. One time I had to go to New York City for some tests. My mom used to hate when my dad drove because he had a heavy foot on the gas pedal. Every time he drove us he kept missing the exit we needed to get off. We must have gone across the George Washington Bridge fifty times before we found that exit. Mom and I were sitting in the back crossing our fingers!

Every time I heard the phrase "George Washington Bridge," I would just laugh to my mom and make an ugly face for her. She knew what I meant. It was funny for us, but my dad wanted to forget about that damn experience.

*Sixth flashback*: I went up on a Ferris wheel every Fourth of July with my dad. Every summer for the Fourth of July celebration, Atlantic Highlands had a Firemen's Fair at the harbor. I really liked the rides for the children, such as bumper cars, the whip, a Ferris wheel and many others. Every year my dad and mom took me to the fair. When we got near the Ferris wheel, I would say "Dad?" and look back and forth between the Ferris wheel and him; all the while having a big grin on my face. I was laughing, and my dad knew what I was saying. He always took me on the Ferris wheel when I was little. I could not wait until the fair came, just to go on that ride.

The Ferris wheel was the best ride. My dad would take me out of my manual wheelchair and threw me over his shoulder. He would sit next to me, wrap his arms around me and hold me tight. I liked how it felt with the motion of the wheel going up in the air and coming down again. Having the ocean breeze hit me in face, smelling the fresh hot dogs grilling, and seeing the sparkling New York skyline, all made me sit back and relax. When I see Ferris wheels and rides I remember those good old days.

As I looked at my dad lying there in the hospital, those memories flooded back to my mind. Maybe he was thinking about some of them too. Even though those days are long gone, they are never forgotten because I had an incredible dad! There is a saying that all good things must come to an end; I was prepared for that too.

My brother decided to bring our dad home and let him spend his last days with him. Bobby told him that we loved him, and it was okay to go with our mom. On October 23, 2000 our dad went in his sleep peacefully and with a smile on his face.

This was what I wrote about our dad for his mass:
*Frank Ghizzone was a Navy veteran of World War II, serving in the Pacific. He used to tell Bobby about his time there and was proud about it. He led a happy life.*

*I remember how I used to like to tease my dad. I would call my dad and ask him for money. He would say, "you are going to put me in the poor house!" When I was living at their home, my dad and I would watch soap operas together. He used to do anything for me because I was his little girl.*

*That day in the hospital, he said that Bobby was going to take great care of me and everything. Bobby was a good son to him and he is a great brother to me.*

*My dad was a kind-hearted, loving, and good father. He was kind to everybody that he saw. Everybody that knew him misses him, but especially Bobby and me. He left Bobby and me behind to go on to live our own happy lives. He is with his dad, mom, sisters, brothers, ex-wife Dolly, and our loving mom, thank you!*

As I am writing this chapter about my dad, it has been 17 years ago he left this world! I remember him doing many things that most dads would not do with their disabled child, such as going on a Ferris wheel, holding their disabled child over their head and letting them fall into a swimming pool,  figuring out how to go for a sled ride, and having as many life experiences as possible with your disabled child.

That was my life with my dad! I love you, Dad, and thanks for the memories!

# Finding work

When I graduated from college, I wanted to work somewhere near where I live in Monmouth County, and at a place I could feel successful. My limitations are real in terms of what I can do with my body in the work force, but my mind operates at the speed of light! I'm not able to speak on my own. What I have that allows me to communicate to people is an augmentative alternative communication device called a Pathfinder. I can access my Pathfinder by clicking a switch with my knee. I can say anything that I want to. It takes a lot of skills and patience. With lots of effort, I can manage to get my thoughts across to people. Sometimes I even give speeches out in the community about what I can do.

I really feel that you won't find my list of abilities in any job description. I love children, so I was trained to read stories with my Pathfinder. Also, I can do circle time with handouts I make at home with my PC. I can do research assignments and talk about them with my Pathfinder to the children. I wrote all those things on my resume. I sent my resume to various child care facilities and school systems, and I even sent a letter to the board of education. Maybe I got three responses. First school: although I was more than qualified, it was not accessible for my wheelchair. Second school: my transportation couldn't take me there. I had some luck with a third school: I had to do some paper work and the board would need to approve me to be a substitute teacher. But they didn't get back to me either.

17

Not one school asked me, would you like to come in for an interview?

I feel they didn't want to accommodate me because of my limitations. That is a shame! My feeling is, the children they are educating need to see somebody who is like me in their school. That would enable them to have more respect for physically challenged people in their community. Most children don't know what to think when they see somebody in a wheelchair and especially one who has a speech impairment. What better place to teach them how to overcome their fears and answer questions they have, than in our schools? Some schools integrate physical challenged children into their school systems. I truly feel the public schools should integrate disabled teachers as well. The nondisabled students can see that disabled teachers are capable of teaching too. In short, it would be beneficial for all students to see physically challenged people working in the school system.

The job hunt is hard for just about everybody. It is extremely difficult when you are disabled in a power chair and using a communication device. Employers should have an open mind and show some compassion and creativity. People who are in wheelchairs can work as well as anybody else. That said, people with disabilities might need some different kinds of accommodation to do their work. For example, widening the work areas (such as doorways and aisles), adapting their computer to make it easier for them to use, and removing objects in their way to make it easier for them to move around by themselves.

I believe some employers would see people with disabilities can work like them, but they might have a different way of producing the work. Of course those employers might learn patience and have some compassion for the people with disabilities outside of work.

I graduated from Brookdale community college and I am very bright! Nevertheless, employers wouldn't give me a chance. They only saw my power chair and my communication device. Right away they weren't interested in what I could do for them.

Ever since I was 3 years old I went to school at the Schroth School. From when I turned 21 until now I have gone to Ladacin Network. Ladacin stands for Lifetime Assistance for Developmental and Challenging Individual Needs. They serve people with different kinds of disabilities. Their mission is teaching their students, clients and residents to become as independent as possible in their lives.

Ladacin Network speech department and AAC Specialists trained me on a voice output augmentative and alternative communication device. Back then I was using a switch that

I clicked with my knee to control the blinking lights on my communication device's screen, so I could choose the words that I wanted to say. This was called a scanning selection technique.

Plus, I volunteered in child care for years and was recognized as a great worker. All the time, people would come up to me and tell me how great I was using a communication device with my knee. The speech therapists taught me how to program it. I programmed children books into my Pathfinder and read to the childcare children.

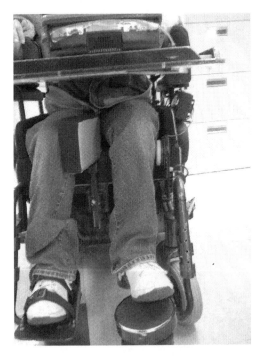

I was an ambassador for Prentke Romich Company (manufacturer for the Pathfinder) for years. I went around to different places and gave speeches about my Pathfinder.

I give demonstrations how I use my Pathfinder and the audiences were always amazed. I volunteered for a museum directing children where to go and to be careful in the museum. I also mentored a teenager over the internet. He used and still uses a Pathfinder too.

Then I remembered somebody advised me that I might have to 'sell' myself to get a job, and that was I did. One fateful day, I asked the director of Ladacin if I could talk to her. We made an appointment to talk. I went home and started to prepare what I wanted to say to her on my Pathfinder. I was a student, client, tech client, resident; willing to help anybody who asked me at Ladacin Network. I was determined, and wrote down my reasons why Ladacin should hire me.

People generally were amazed by how well I did, and by my list of skills, but unfortunately, they still wouldn't offer me a job. Often I had proven to Ladacin my communication skills and what I was capable of doing for them. I knew that Ladacin could adapt anything for my needs. It was time for them to adapt a job for my needs.

Often prospective employers would tell me that "change is good for you, Denise!"

I asked the director how Ladacin could help me, because I felt my situation was different from other clients. Most clients can use their hands to do certain jobs in the community such as copying things for a company, stuffing envelopes, shredding old documents, and packaging things. I can't do any of those things. So, I gave some suggestions to her about what I could do by myself on my Pathfinder. She listened to me. She asked me questions, and I answered them truthfully with my Pathfinder. I asked if Ladacin could accommodate me with a job because I wanted to be productive and helpful.

I asked the director: if you don't hire me, who would? I told her about my experiences going on interviews. The employers thought I was talented, but they didn't take the extra step to hire me. If I could handle college then I could handle a job. I just needed a chance! She said she would see what she could do. On my second interview I brought in my portfolio to show her. At the time I was in a project to help me to get a job with my Pathfinder. This program taught me how to make a professional portfolio with my certificates, recognitions, and diploma. I wrote my resume myself. I was trained how to present myself on an interview using my Pathfinder. After the training was completed, I took a deep breath of relief. I told myself, it is over! I started to look for a job like anybody else does!

In 2006, Ladacin created a unique job for me. Now I am a teacher with both the Child Care and Speech departments. In Child Care, I lead circle time, read stories, and do projects on my Pathfinder. I also make my own work sheets on my computer at home. The children just love when I come in to teach them. I think it is a very good idea for me to work with little children. The children need the exposure to people who are in wheelchairs and use communication devices effectively. When they see me trying to talk, they may be encouraged to try harder to accomplish things in life. I have been told I am an excellent role model.

With the Speech department, I encourage the children and adults to use their communication devices. I do small groups with the disabled students. I teach them how important it is to speak up for themselves, and how important it is for them to tell somebody when they need help during the day.

My coworkers and I take some of the students out in the community and give speeches to the elementary, middle, high schools, and some colleges. We talk about disabled awareness to the students and teachers. Most of our students communicate with their communication devices.

Even though I am very bright and have a lot to offer people, and have an Associate degree in English from Brookdale Community College, it took me years to find a job. No one wanted to go that extra step to hire me. I'm not sure why (I do have some ideas), but the bottom line is they just didn't. The way I look at it, it is their loss! By reading this chapter, I hope you can see that there are lots of things I can do for Ladacin in spite of my limitations. I go around in my power chair and use my communication device to do my job. My job makes me feel like a person because my coworkers see what I can do, and they are never concerned about my power chair or my communication device.

Ladacin's mission is to help our students and adults to be independent as possible. All employers should have a similar mindset when it comes to people with disabilities. We have feelings and are very intelligent too. We can contribute a lot to just about any workplace!

I am living proof of what a person with a disability can do in spite of all my limitations. As the years go on, my physical limitations are getting worse, but so far I still have my job thanks to new technology and supportive co-workers and management.

## Guest speaker at Point Pleasant Boro

I am very excited about the story I am telling in this chapter because I arranged this event with my brother's friend by myself. This little event turned out to be a huge and exciting event that everybody involved would remember the rest of their lives. Hopefully, the students took something away from what I spoke on. Looking back on that day not just the students, but even the teachers, parents, and community learned something from me about all I can do being in a power chair. I utilized a communication device just by my knee to give a speech. Also, as a teacher, of course I have important and valuable experiences to speak on that can benefit everybody who hears about them.

Every time I think of September 2012, I am so proud of myself. It was a highlight of my life! The other people were surprised how well I conducted myself. To this day people are still talking about my presentation.

During the summer of 2012, my brother went to his friend's wedding. My brother was talking to another friend who knew me. He asked my brother "How is your sister doing?" My brother told him everything I was doing: "She's a teacher and goes out to public schools and delivers these incredible speeches with her communication device. She is great, and she makes people really think." His friend asked my brother if I would come to his High

25

School to speak to his students. My brother gave him my email address to contact me. What follows explains how this amazing event evolved into an outstanding accomplishment for other people to learn from.

Mr. Johnson and I emailed back and forth for a couple of weeks. He explained to me what he was looking for. Basically, they wanted a guest speaker to talk positively about their life with a disability. Right away I wrote him an email and asked what is the date? I thought to myself, I'm going! I am the perfect guest speaker for this topic!

I prepared my speech on my communication device at home. I got a couple editorial comments, and I kept revising my speech. I only had a couple of weeks to get it done. I had made some outstanding speeches in the past, but this speech needed to be better than all of them.

My big day finally arrived. My cousin's company has an accessible van which a driver used to drive me to the Point Boro High. The reason I asked my cousin was because it was less stressful for me than to set up transportation with another company.

Mr. Johnson and some other people were waiting outside for me. Two other coworkers came and met me. Then we walked to the auditorium and got my communication device up and ready. I waited for Mr. Johnson to introduce me. Beforehand I had emailed my speech to them so that they could put it on the screen above me. That way they could follow along while I was saying my speech because there were 500 people in the auditorium to hear my speech.

When I heard my name from Mr. Johnson, I came out from behind the curtain and began my speech:

> **Hi, my name is Denise Ghizzone. I work for Ladacin Network. It is a real honor to be here today. I would like to thank Mr. Johnson for asking me to come to speak at your school.**

*I usually go to the elementary schools to talk about me and the disabled community. This device in front of me is called a Pathfinder. It is a voice output augmentative and alternative communication device. It is a fast and easy way to communicate with people. It is computer based and with it I can say anything that I desire. There are blinking lights above the pictures. I am using a switch positioned on my wheelchair that I click with my knee to control the lights. This is called a scanning selection technique. That is okay, this is just a computer. I am using a vocabulary program called unity or min speak. Sequences of pictures retrieve different words. Such as, the symbols INTERJECTION and PHONE represent, 'hello.' I think there are 3000 words and different phrases that I can choose from. It is not really that difficult, but you need your memory to remember the picture codes. If I forget the picture codes I can also spell using my Pathfinder. I just happened to prepare today's message ahead of time using the notebook feature.*

*I have had amazing speech-language pathologists over the years. They taught me how to be excellent at using my Communication devices. Also, I would like to let you know, I had some amazing teachers, occupational therapists and a network of friends throughout the years. They worked with me to get my resume, cover letter and portfolio done. Also, they taught me some extra skills to go on an interview with using my Communication device. They told me, I can do anything when I put my mind to something. I had some incredible parents, too. They fought to get me into Brookdale Community College and they knew I had a great mind to offer people. They were right, I have a lot to offer. Every day I miss them so much. I had three goals I set for myself over the years. I went to college and I did great. At first, they weren't too accommodating, but my mom pushed them to take me. She told them I was very intelligent and a hard worker. So, they took me. It was very challenging to me and I loved going to Brookdale. I did all my work myself with physical assistance. It took me*

*12 long years to graduate, and successfully I finally did! That was my dream: to go to college, and I accomplished that goal. A mind is a terrible thing to waste. It blows my mind when non-disabled people look down at themselves because they aren't pretty, smart, or even because somebody is mad at them. Well those things are not worth stressing over. The way I view things, if you can talk, taking care of yourself and walking, you have everything. I watch the news, these days the children are getting bullied for no reason; I would like to know why. Are people that mean to each other these days? That is not good at all. Just listen to me and you will see what I must deal with, all kinds of people each day. Imagine if you have to depend on somebody to take care of you with everything. Let me tell you, that isn't fun at all. That is depressing! I have had cerebral palsy for 44 years. I would like to be able to talk and walk, but I can't. I have to make the best of it. I can accept myself for who I am. Most disabled people can't accept themselves for who they are. I think I could have been a lot worse off than I am right now. I have an older brother named Bobby. He treats me like anybody else. I remember once, when I was watching TV, he turned the channel on purpose, and then he just left. He knew I couldn't get up to change the channel. For that I got him back, I used to knock over his Lincoln logs buildings that he worked on for hours. He hated me for that. We fought a lot like any brother and sister growing up.*

*Well, anyhow, the biggest problem that I found and overcame was finding work. Some employers took one look at me, they didn't know what to do with me. The employers didn't want to take the time out to see what I was capable of doing for them. They even read my portfolio, but they still weren't interested. Once they looked at me, they weren't too sensitive to my needs. They looked at my portfolio and told me they would call me, but they never did. They said that I had talent. I said to myself, can I please have a job! They said that they would get back to me. I thought they didn't treat me very fairly. They didn't ask me anything.*

*So, I was waiting for the places to call me; nobody did. Some employers today should give the disabled population some respect. They should look beyond the disability, and they should be considerate. They also should have an open mind. All I am saying is, the unknown is scary, but the outcome might be worthwhile to the employers.*

*Somebody advised me that you have to know somebody to get a job and sell yourself. My second goal was getting a job. I presented to Ladacin Network all my capabilities and how I can help them. They created the most unique job description for me, and no one could fill those shoes but me! I am the only one who uses a communication device with my knee using a switch and uses a wheelchair with my foot. I asked Ladacin if you won't hire me, how do you expect somebody else would. They didn't have an answer for that question. A month later, I was hired. I am a talented and determined person, to say the least! I used to work in child care; for Ladacin Network with the physically challenged students. I read stories and do projects on my Pathfinder. The children just love when I come in to teach them. The non-disabled children need the exposure to people who are in wheelchairs and use communication devices effectively. When they see me trying to talk, they may try harder to accomplish things in their life. I also work with the speech department. I encourage the disabled children and adults to use their communication devices. I do small group with them. I teach them how to be like me and how to speak up for themselves. I also teach some of the disabled teenagers, they are a lot of fun and I really enjoy teaching them. I teach them how important it is to speak up for themselves, and how important it is for them to tell somebody when they need help during the day. These students are very much like me, but sometimes I have to be hard on them. Sometimes they don't want to use their communication devices. I share with them what it is like out there in the world. If they want to be understood by others, they need to use their communication devices like me. Sometimes they don't like what I am saying, because sometimes life is hard for the disabled people. We have to let people know what our capabilities are, every day. So, you see, even though I can't walk and talk, I can work just like anybody else does. It gives me great pride to be able to work. I take my job seriously, but sometimes I take it too seriously. I love my job and I am willing to help anybody. I started out reading to child care, but I can do a lot more than that.*

*Also, I go out in the public schools and educate the students and the teachers about me and the disabled. People have to look beyond the wheelchairs and communication devices; they are real people just like you. Some of the disabled people want to be sociable to people, but they can't. Or maybe they are very social but not academic enough. People need to get to know them and what their capacities are. Some of the disabled population are aware of people who are making fun of them in the community, and others are not aware. Disabled people have to deal with a great deal on a daily basis; most people aren't aware of that. As for myself, I too have to deal with a lot every day, but I somehow keep my smile on and just accomplish what I need to do. You have to realize, when you see somebody in a wheelchair, don't assume they aren't smart. And don't assume they can't understand you. Most disabled people are offended by how people approach them out in the public. We get talked to very loudly and ignorantly. We are the same as anybody else. When you approach somebody in a wheelchair, stand in front of us and please don't touch our equipment. Be kind and talk to us. Don't judge a person just by what you see in front of you. You are missing a lot if you do that. We might be as intelligent as your best friend. Don't be concerned by what you see from the outside because the inside is what really matters.*

*Transportation is a big hassle. If you want to go somewhere, you can go in your cars or get somebody to take you. When we need to go anywhere, we have to call a special bus company with a wheelchair lift to book a ride one week in advance. I like to go to the beach, mall, restaurants, food shopping, and of course work. I must plan one week in advance to go. That is discouraging, but that is how it is. For example, to come to Point Pleasant Borough High School today, I had to make special arrangements.*

*With everything I shared with you today, there are still a lot of people who aren't aware about the disabled community. I want you to think about and take this message with you today: what if you wouldn't be able to walk and talk? How would you feel being disabled and not getting around to do the things you love? How would it feel to always have to rely on somebody to help you all the time? How would you like to be treated if you were in a wheelchair? Would you be depressed if you became disabled like me? All those questions are ones that you really need to answer and then start rethinking your life. Take the time out of your busy life and get to know some disabled people. Just think about your very best friends and how you treat them. Then you will know how to treat disabled people. I have a nondisabled friend and her name is Karen Rogers and she has boys. She used to work for me at Brookdale and we became friends. She is my best friend. Now we both share 28 years of friendship. She treats me like anybody else. We disagree all the time. We also believe that in life people disagree and that's nothing to get upset over. Life is too short to get mad at people. Everybody should treat people with kindness and respect. I have known her children for that long, too. Now they are adults and they treat me like anybody else. They used to call me Aunt Denise and they still do. They also know how to get to me, ha ha ha. I think of them as my nephews. They are wonderful to me. When they were little, I took them to Disney World. We had a blast together. My best friend and I go to Atlantic City to hang out. Just recently we went to see Boyz II Men. We had a blast together.*

*I have a lot of nondisabled friends. I even hang out with some of my coworkers at the mall and just chill out on the weekends. That is a lot of fun. One of my coworker's son is my buddy and he used to be in child care. Zachary knows how to talk to me. He's 7 years old. He helps me shop. I met a lot of kids in child care and I keep in touch with some of them. Some kids really bonded with me. This one boy made me really think from the start. Colin was too smart for his own good. He was very special to me because he always remembered the right name to call my communication device. He was only 5 and he used to say "your communication device." He was amazing at five years old. I still see him every once in a while. He gives me hugs when he sees me. Some kids are not afraid of people with disability at all.*

*You see, whatever you want to do you can do no matter how far out it is. You can do anything if you just put your mind to do something and stick to it. It might be a long time but at the end you will say that Miss Denise Ghizzone was right all along. It was a real honor speaking to everybody here at Point Pleasant Boro High, and I want to thank you for allowing me the opportunity to come today. Enjoy your day!*

While I presented this speech, all the students and faculties were in awe and by the end there wasn't a dry eye in the auditorium. You could have heard a pin drop. All of them paid attention to me and got a lot out of it. Being respectful, sensitive -- and regardless what is on the outside -- getting to know people from their inside is what truly counts. My point was that everybody should be treated the same as anybody else! It shouldn't matter if they are in a wheelchair or not.

When I was finished, I got a standing ovation! I felt that I had outdone myself once again with my speech. The local newspaper was there to interview me and take my picture. The students and faculties came up to congratulate me.

I had a great time and will remember that the rest of my life. As for Point Borough High, I hope they will remember that assembly for years to come!

## My operation

One day in my 40s, I couldn't sit up by myself. I was in horrible neck pain. I wasn't myself after that. The people at my apartment noticed I couldn't sit up or push myself anymore. I told my brother and my friend Karen that something was wrong with me. Somebody from my apartment building took me to the emergency room.

Of course, I knew this was due to the fact of my cerebral palsy, and it only happened occasionally, but that didn't make it any easier to deal with the fact that my head kept moving uncontrollably. That caused a lot of strain on my neck. That was how it was. There was nothing I could do to stop my movements. The pain was so bad that I couldn't push myself in my manual wheelchair backwards; in fact, that was impossible to do. Nobody knows what really happened to me. Maybe I had a mini stroke or maybe my body gave out all of a sudden. This was one of those situations you ask yourself why and have no answers.

Unfortunately, the doctors and nurses in the emergency room weren't any help because they didn't know what was wrong with me. The doctors and the nurses needed to be trained how to deal with people with disabilities. They didn't want to touch or stand too close to me. The people who work in the medical field or emergency rooms need to understand that people who are in wheelchairs need to be treated like anybody else. Please don't assume they can't answer for themselves. They may be intelligent as you. Or they could be an Author like me ha ha ha, you can never know who is sitting in a wheelchair! People with disabilities are human beings and should be treated the same as everybody else. I know I was not taken good care of in the emergency room that day. Everybody needs some compassion for people with disabilities because we can have a heart attack, stroke, or some other disease the same as everybody else in this world. I know people with disabilities who got those illnesses and their outcome was not very good.

I went to my doctor and he wanted me to go for some tests. I went back and forth to get tests, MRI, CAT scans. My brother took me back and forth to so many doctors and all the kinds of tests I had to get.

Doctor after doctor just looked at me and asked me "what's wrong with you?" My brother explained I had cerebral palsy and my neck was hurting me. I wasn't myself. I went to several different doctors but no help.

The nurse from my apartment found me a different doctor that specialized in spines and necks. His name is Dr. Yalamanchili. He is a very nice doctor and he cares. I saw that when he walked into the room because he shook my hand. The doctor shook my hand and I said to myself he is my hero! Finally, a doctor who wasn't afraid of me. My brother was grateful to him. My brother and I knew he was the one that could make me better again.


I really liked the spinal doctor. Everybody told me I should get a second opinion, so I did; but I once I had done so, I said "No I want Yalamanchili!" I went back to him and he said I either needed an operation on my neck or I needed to take a lot of medicines. I said I would go for the operation. I was thinking I was in too much pain to go on anyhow. I just wanted to get it over with. I was very scared because I had never had an operation before. I would either be fine or be with my parents up in heaven. Either way I wouldn't be in pain! I had my brother, his girlfriend and of course Karen. Everybody was coming to see me before my operation. I didn't look myself and they thought I wasn't going to make it. They had no confidence in me that I would make it. I was determined that I would pull through and then I would be myself again.


As the operation day approached, I thought "This is not going to be the end for me" because I had decided three important things I wanted to do before I leave this world: I wanted to graduate from college and I did that in 1999! I wanted a job and in 2006 I was employed at Ladacin Network. I needed to do just one more thing and very important thing that I worked hard on throughout my life. That was to write my life story. The operation wasn't in my plan. I told myself I am going to write one way or the other, so I would find a way to use my computer again. I was thinking of my stories collected in binders in my filing cabinet throughout the years. I thought: "I'm going to do something with them if it is the last thing I do." I was determined to get back to my usual self somehow.

Anyhow, Karen stayed with me the night before my big day. My best friend; she's still with me throughout everything. She is a breast cancer survivor too.

We had had some difficult times when she had cancer, but she had beaten cancer. I was her biggest supporter. And now I knew she was going to help me through this. We promised each other we are going to live. I think she was the only one who believed I was going to make it. There was a time even I didn't think I would make it while waiting for my operation. It was rough on me physically and emotionally. I was too tired to hear anything people were saying. At one point somebody told me I couldn't have the operation! I burst out crying! I thought about what my brother and Karen had said, and I said I'm going to have the operation no matter what. After that I wasn't going to listen to anybody else on the subject again.

January 15 – operation day -- finally came. Karen got me ready for my operation and we went to the hospital. We waited for my brother and his girlfriend. Karen put me on the bed and Dr. Yalamanchili came in. I had a big smile for him. He asked me if I was ready for him and I said I was. I had a flash back to the time in his office when he told me what he was going to do. He told me my discs were bad in my neck. He was going to replace them with screws and metal. That's exactly what he did. I had to get a blood transfusion in the course of the operation.

The operation took nine hours, but I came out of it just great! I was on a lot of medicine, so I was "out of it" most of the time. I had to wear a neck brace and I was on a ventilator for a couple days.

I saw a lot of the doctors, and various friends and family came to see me. I kept thinking to myself, "I am still alive!" I was thinking of my parents; I said to myself "Damn, I guess they didn't want me up there to bother them yet; well, thanks Mom and Dad." I figured they wanted me to keep dealing with these people down here. Why me?!

I stayed in the hospital for a few days. I was happy once I was out of it because I don't like hospitals. In thinking back to the operation, I said to myself "Where was Dr. Yalamanchili?" I was too out of it to remember he had been there. I was disappointed that I didn't remember him being there because I really liked him. Oh damn, finally I had a man that I really liked, and I couldn't remember seeing him taking care of me. That was just my luck!

Then I was moved to rehab, and I didn't like that at all. Once I came to myself, I wanted to go home. Then I saw somebody that used to work with me a long time prior to meeting there. She remembered me too, and that helped me feel better.

Some of the doctors and the nurses needed to be trained in how to talk to disabled people. The doctors were making me mad because they were asking me what my name was. I thought to myself, don't you know I'm nonverbal? One doctor asked me what today's date was. Of course, I cheated by looking at the board in the room. He apparently didn't know it was on the board. I just laughed to myself.

Every day the nurses put ice water in front of me, and then just left. I was happy to see Karen that day because she gave me a drink; and my brother did too. The nurses told Karen that I was not going to the bathroom. Karen asked them if they were helping me with my drink, because I needed some help. I looked at Karen and she knew they weren't helping me with drinking. She told them I needed to drink a lot to go to the bathroom. Karen knew I was mad. I told Karen I wanted to go home with her and she laughed. I was feeling like myself and that it was time to go. It turned out I had to stay for another few weeks. I didn't like the food and I couldn't go to the bathroom. That sucked! I couldn't take a shower; that really got to me.

I convinced Karen to bring me a McDonald's fish sandwich and soda! After eating the sandwich and going to the bathroom, I felt better.

Later on, they took me downstairs for therapies. I wasn't in the mood to go to therapies. It was quite amusing, but I wasn't in the mood to laugh. The occupational therapist told me I could feed myself. I thought she was crazy. I just looked and smiled! I said to myself "where is Karen and my brother when I need them?!"

My friend Karen

The rehab stressed me out. I knew my arms and hands wouldn't be the same again. I can't remember even one of my doctors saying my arms and legs wouldn't be the same again. They only said I might need pain management.

Oh, no pain management, I thought. I didn't want to be on a lot of medicines because that was not me at all. I had a plan to get back to my job, to get a power chair and a new communication device so I could use my computer at home. People told me I needed to relax and find new things to do. I just smiled at them and said to myself that is fine for you, but I just wanted to use my computer and to do the same things I had been doing before. Relaxing is one thing that is impossible for me to do.

A number of times I rode in the ambulance to see Dr. Yalamanchili from rehab. I was happy to get out of rehab for a while. I was so happy to see him again. He took some X-rays of my neck.

Then my big day was finally here: going home! I didn't think the day would ever come. I had a big smile for everybody at rehab. I said to myself "I'm not coming here again!" Hell no!

When I got home, I was excited to see all the staff who took care of me at my apartment. They were glad to see me back and feeling better. And I was so happy to be home again. I made it through my first operation without any problem! I reflected that it really wasn't that bad.

First of all I ate and went to the bathroom. After that I felt better. I sat in the recliner and watched TV for a while. Then I did what I had been dreaming about for weeks: I slept in my own bed. In the morning I took a hot shower. I was fine after that.

For a month or so after that I had to sit in a recliner until I got my strength back again to use my chair. That meant I couldn't go out at all for that time. Of course, I didn't get back all the way to how I was previously, but I had to deal with that. I didn't like it, but I realized I could have been a lot worse off. First, my plan was to get off the medicines that made me sleepy. I needed to be alert if I wanted to drive a power chair and use a communication device again. I must say I was a terrible patient when I was recovering. I did what I had to do to get myself together. I still had my stubbornness in me.

I had to put this black machine around my neck to heal my neck. It was pretty neat. I had a nurse, occupational therapist, and physical therapist come to see me two or three times a week for two months. The nurse changed the dressing on my neck. The physical therapist and occupational therapist gave me exercises for my arms and my legs. Everybody was telling me I was doing a good job, but I knew this wouldn't help me do what I wanted to do. I still felt weak and drained. I wasn't myself for a few months.

## My ways of communicating

Oh yes, my recovery was difficult to do. I overcame so many challenges in my life. From the various teachers and speech therapists I had over the years I learned how to read and use communication devices. Let me help you understand how I overcame those earlier challenges.

Taking you back to the famous book *Dick and Jane*. Do you remember *Dick and Jane*? My teachers drilled it into my head and showed me the words in the book, so I could recognize the words later. All my teachers gave me harder words to expand my vocabulary and I learned to memorize them. They gave me flash cards with words. Eventually I learned how to type with a typewriter. I used to type using the words on the flash cards over, over, and over again. That was how I learned to spell, by copying the flash cards with the typewriter.

The typewriter was well and good, but not a very efficient way for me to write. Then came the late 80's with new communication devices; I had a couple of them. My life really started when I had them. Let me tell you about what a difference they made for me.

When I was 22, I had some amazing Augmentative and Alternative Communication (AAC) specialists at Ladacin come into my life. One saw me with my headpointer on. She said to herself, this woman needs a different way to communicate.

The AAC specialists trained me on Minspeak with pictures. I didn't like it. There were all kinds of pictures on the communication device, but no words or letters. Really, I thought she was crazy, because there I was -- an adult talking with pictures. Somehow, I smiled through it. Eventually, I understood what the pictures meant. Then I was evaluated, and they trained me on a Liberator voice-out augmentative and alternative communication device. The Liberator worked the same as the Pathfinder I described to you in an earlier chapter.

The Liberator has blinking lights above the pictures. I was using a switch positioned on my wheelchair that I clicked with my knee to control the lights. This is called a scanning selection technique.

When I was in my late twenties, my AAC specialist hooked my communication device up with my computer at home. I bought the infrared device for my computer to interact with my communication device. The infrared component is a square box. It is a transmitter to my computer from my communication device. Whatever I wanted to do, the infrared sent signals to my computer and my computer would do it. Basically, my communication device was my keyboard and mouse using the infrared device.

As the years went on, I went to Temple University to learn more about controlling the computer with my communication device. I loved that and learned everything I could. Now I am an expert at it. The person who worked in the program came to my apartment and taught me how to work my computer easier with my communication device.

I was taught how to program my communication device to give commands for my computer. For example, I could close out a window, get to my E mail, and go to the Start button all by pressing one or two buttons. That was hard to learn, but it's been incredibly useful throughout the years. I am much faster at the computer with those skills. I can do more things with the computer now than when the technology come out. I'm not limited to a couple of commands. I can do anything like anybody else can. Twenty years later, I still remember those skills and have added many more that I have discovered for myself. They came in handy. Here's one example: I discovered I love taking a selfie. I can take videos of myself on my computer!

Unfortunately, my scanning days were over when I had the operation on my neck. My knee doesn't work anymore like it used to. I was mad and frustrated, but all good things must come to end. It's a part of life!

My speech therapist found and got an eye gaze communication device for somebody else. I saw it and was awed by it. Since I had had my Pathfinder forever by then, I was eligible to get a new communication device. That time I was preparing to have my operation on my neck. I was thinking that by the time I was myself again, my new communication device would be there.

I went from scanning with my knee for years and now I am using my eyes! It is called an Eyegaze Echo 2. My communication device picks up my eyes on the black part on the bottom of my communication device. It shows me where I'm looking on the screen.

The Eyegaze Echo 2 works the same as my Pathfinder. All I must do is focus on the pictures so that I can create sentences. The technology out there is out of this world. Now, Bluetooth works the same as the infrared transmitter between my computer and my communication device. I was set with my communication device and computer again. Right back where I left off before the operation!

I am a perfect example of an early adopter for new technology. I had a Liberator and then Pathfinder. I used to scan for years. Now I am using the eye gaze communication device.

Therefore, all teachers and speech therapists should try to teach your students and clients to read. Pictures alone won't help them in their life. Without reading they can't be successful. If you can't read, you can't do your job. Plus, from a disabled person's perspective I am proud to read. I wouldn't be here today and do what I do without reading. I wouldn't be able to spell, work, use a computer or write a book without reading. I truly believe all children with disabilities should be taught how to read, recognize their letters and some sounds. Nobody knows what it is going on in their head when they are nonverbal. People with a disability have the right to be treated like anybody else in this world. As for me, I learned how to spell and read just by my teachers taking the time out to teach me. With that I became the intelligent woman I am now.

The English language is difficult to learn, but I rely on my sight mostly. I have my tricks that I have learned over the years. For example, not being able to talk means I can't hear all the sounds in a word. Take the words 'hear' and 'here'; they sound the same, but there are different ways to spell those words. I learned that the word 'hear' has the word 'ear' in it. Therefore, I remember the correct spelling by thinking "people hear with their ears." The word 'there' has the word 'here' in it. I now know the differences between those words. I know 'where' from 'wear.' Where is a question word. All the question words start with 'WH.'

Also, teachers and speech therapists need to keep in mind different ways to access your student's or client's communication devices. You never know if one method will work forever. Just trust me on this one: you don't know what is going to happen to students and clients over time. It would be a very good idea if you tried at least two different access methods with them. You might want to try scanning with a switch or eye gaze machine yourself, because then you will know how it feels. Those are tough technologies to master. It isn't easy to sit still and just move your eyes around for a couple minutes. It's more tiring than you may think. You must focus on one picture at a time before you can move on.

Throughout my life, even though I had a disability I was not different from regular children in other ways. For example, I still had to learn how to read and spell. It took me longer, but I managed. Having a disability made it harder to find the best and fastest ways to do things; but nothing is impossible these days. As I got older, my physical needs started to change because first I used a headpointer and then my knee to communicate. With new technologies, I can use my eyes to communicate and I am still doing what I loved before: USING MY COMPUTER!

The right way to treat people with disabilities

Throughout this book is a message for everybody to think about and hopefully to use in their life: the way people with disabilities should be treated in this world. I am a teacher with a physical disability, so I am very aware how other people perceive me at first!

Many years ago, I wrote this article at Brookdale and it describes how people need to treat people with any disabilities.

## Persons with Disabilities
## A unique culture

By Denise Ghizzone

Because there are so many different cultures in this world, it is hard to experience every culture. Some cultures result from race, ethnicity, and gender. As we mature, we might belong to a new culture based on our hobbies, income, education, etc. We also might try to deny certain cultures that we were born into.

These are the most common cultures that people are aware of, but what about those people who have disabilities? They are unique in their beliefs and the way they see and handle life experiences.

I strongly believe there is a "Persons with Disabilities" culture. As for me, I have a physical disability. I can't walk, talk, or physically take care of myself. In addition, there are some disabilities that you can't see; for example, some called learning disabilities.

People with disabilities have their own beliefs and a certain unique way that they achieve things. They must follow them because they can't physically do it any other way. Also, they have their own customs, which come natural to them.

Here are some examples of the prejudices and stereotypes in our society that a person with a disability faces. 1. If somebody is sitting in a wheelchair, you assume that they have a disability, or that the person is unaware of their environment. 2. When a person in a wheelchair has an alphabet board or communication device in front of them, you assume they are learning the alphabet.

3. When you see a person with dark glasses walking a dog, you assume that they are blind. 4. When a person is slow at learning to read, you assume they aren't interested in reading. 5. When a person can't spell, you will jump to the conclusion that they aren't paying attention.

People who are nonverbal are accustomed to talking with communication devices, body language, or with an alphabet board. People who are blind have dogs to see for them. Some people can't grasp reading because they have a learning disability that affects their comprehension to read. Also, they have trouble with spelling. A person without a disability cannot experience this culture because they don't understand how difficult it is to have a positive attitude when faced with their challenges. It is a totally different culture and that comes naturally to people with disabilities.

Other people can talk with their mouth and it comes natural to them. People are accustomed to sitting or standing. People can see where they are walking.

People with disabilities have strong beliefs because they can't give up on believing. They have a different outlook on life because most of them are in wheelchairs. They take pride in achieving the "little things" such as learning to eat by themselves or writing their name for the first time. A lot of people with disabilities work for a living and are proud. Their inner strength believes in what their capabilities are.

Also, they have dreams about their life. Dreaming helps them to cope with things in society. For example, you can dream without any physical movement. You don't need to rely on somebody to help or anything. Dreams are private because you can be anything in a dream.

Persons with disabilities value things others take for granted. They need things more than an average person does. They need material things such as wheelchairs, communication devices and computers. They value people because people help with their needs. For example, getting around because they need special transportation like a lift or a big trunk for their wheelchair. They must plan their activities ahead of time. It is easy for other people to get a ride.

Knowing how to communicate with a person who is nonverbal is very important to understand. The easiest way to converse is to give them yes or no questions. Don't talk down to them because you never know how much they understand. You might hurt their feelings. Talk to them the way that you would want to be addressed, if you were in their situation. You may find a new friendship by just having a conversation.

These individuals are accustomed to living a certain way and they don't know how to live any other way. Outside of this norm looking in, people make the wrong assumptions, which make them feel embarrassed. These days you can't assume what is right because you don't really know the person's situation. We all interpret things differently. We can learn by asking questions not to take it upon ourselves to make the wrong assumptions. The right answers are right there in front of you. Most people may feel uncomfortable to ask questions but asking helps you to know more. You get a better understanding of how people live their lives.

I believe doctors, nurses, teachers, and employers should meet people with disabilities. They should talk to them. They need to take some time out of their busy lives and have some conversations with them. Then they will know that they can't assume things simply by seeing their power chair or communication devices. They may look like they can't do anything for themselves but take it from me, that is not always the case. Take me, for example; I am in a power chair and use a communication device to communicate. I am a teacher with a communication device, too. I go out in the schools to educate the teachers and students. I can do a lot for myself, but I am treated unfairly by the doctors and the nurses or whoever thinks they know me just by looking at me from the outside. Remember the inside is what counts!

I hope this article will clear up any misconceptions about persons with disabilities. People with disabilities are human beings, not people to be overlooked. They can breathe, watch everything that others do, and can love people such as you. What counts is what is on the inside of people with a disability; that's what matters. We like to be treated with respect and kindness. Everybody needs to be treated like that.

# Coping with what movements I have left

I must say I have had a great life, but some tragic things came up. I thought it was the worst thing ever, when my parents died, but it wasn't. Some people might think that living with a disability is the worst thing ever, but I have to say no, not really! I will say for 45 years I was able to move my body around by myself pretty well without help from anybody. I could move my manual wheelchair with my foot, turn on lights, and work my TV with my hands and do many other little things for myself. My parents used to say if you want something, you need to try your best! Or "Practice makes perfect!"

By the time I was an adult, TV remotes came out. I could press the buttons with my fingers. In my way and with some practice I could turn on the TV for myself. Eventually, Ladacin's rehab tech and my occupational therapist made me a remote holder with a handle for my remote control, so I could pick it up from the TV stand to my tray. I felt I was independent doing those tasks. They made a holder for my remote control for the air conditioner. They built a stand for one of my flat screen TVs. They made me a stand for my communication device in front of my computer. Those were little things I used to treasure for myself. I managed lifting my hand up and turning on and off the lights in my apartment. I was so proud of that accomplishment. I was just thinking the people who built these apartments should put the light switches lower because – hello?! -- we are in wheelchairs. People with disabilities can't reach that high for the light switches on the wall.

All those little things that I used to do for myself such as turning on the light, changing the channels on the TV, and many more other things people take for granted for themselves, I was so proud doing for myself. Now my favorite saying is, all good things must come to an end! I really get mad at people who tell me when they had a hard day, or their life is not going the way they want. I wish and would love to have those problems!

Just picture this: in the winter it starts getting dark at 5:00 in the afternoon and you can't turn on the lights for yourself; what should you do? Or you want to see your favorite show on TV and you can't turn on the TV by yourself; again, what should you do?

I always wondered how do people cope with losing their mobilities from a stroke? For years they are used to doing certain everyday tasks. One day they can't do them anymore; how would they feel? Imagine having that feeling, and you can't go back in time! After my neck operation, that was the way I felt. I was even more disabled than before, if you can believe that. Even though I was disabled, I still could do some things for myself and felt so proud.

Five years later, I had to accept that my arms and hands had stopped working. I made my legs work a little but not much. I go for botox injections for my arms and hands every 4 months to loosen my muscles. Those injections hurt. What I want to do with my arms and hands I can't do even with the botox injections.

The one thing I can still do as before is this: I am still a teacher. When I got my new communication device and my new power chair, I went back to work. The children in child care and the other teachers were excited to see me, but I was too tired to watch and teach children anymore. It was too hard to work my communication device with my eyes and watch the children at the same time. I moved around in my new power chair with my chin switch and I was scared to run over the children all around me. After volunteering and working in child care so many years, I had to bring that chapter to an end. I needed to stop before some child got hurt because of my power chair.

I had a talk with my bosses and told them I couldn't work in child care any longer. I needed to do something different before I ran some child over with my power chair or a child ran into me and get hurt. They were disappointed, but they understood. My saying is, all good things must come to an end!

I really enjoy working with the disabled teenagers a lot more. I can get my frustrations out on them. Ha ha ha, I am only kidding! They need somebody who can tell them how it is and stick to their word. And that is me; I never back down or go easy on them. Eventually, they will learn by my way. I know all of their tricks because I was like them once upon a time. The other teachers and therapists let them get away with murder! My trick with those teenagers: just don't look into their eyes because their eyes will get to everybody. I used to get my way with my dad all the time when he looked into my eyes.

Another thing that is the same is that I can work my computer the same as before, but with my eyes now. I am thankful for that. I just laughed at people when they told me I needed to take it easy and I needed a new hobby apart from writing! Yeah right, I wasn't going to stop writing as that point in my life. I was on a mission to write my life story and nobody was going to stop me. When I want something, I will go after it and that's what I did. I am going to tell you in a later chapter about how my life dream finally came true.    Becoming an Author!

## My manual and power wheelchairs

When I was 22 or 23, I received my first power chair. The reason I didn't get a power chair when I was younger was that I wasn't interested in having one. That was just my opinion of power chairs, but don't go by me. It seemed to me that power chairs made people lazy sitting in them all day. Now to be fair, I have seen some cute little power chairs. Don't get me wrong; some children need power chairs, but they need to know how to work them and have to use them all of the time because power chairs are hard to get. Most insurance companies might give you a hard time getting one even when a child really needs one. Another insurance company might give a power chair right away to a child. That is why children must utilize them every day. Children and the adults that care for them should have a level of maturity.

As for me, power chairs weren't a big deal. My house was too small to need a power chair anyhow. I was smart and could move my legs just fine. I could move in my manual wheelchair with my leg and foot. Once I pushed backwards into the kitchen with my foot because I wanted to be with my mom. It was much easier going backwards. One day I lifted my footrests and started pushing myself. Since then I pushed myself that way almost 36 years.

My one leg kept getting stronger and stronger, and I kept pushing around in the house. Sometimes I pushed myself outside in front of my house. In my neighborhood, I watched the kids playing near me. I had a blast!

I was in the Special Olympics, in the wheelchair races. I participated in 25 meters, 50 meters, and the slalom. I even won ribbons and medals too. It was a lot of fun. When I got older I wasn't interested in it anymore. I was like most people, it got boring doing the same thing over and over again.

I can't use my hands to drive a power chair, so my therapists, the rehab tech at Ladacin, and the wheelchair vendor invented something to work with my foot. I had a hard time finding the buttons, I looked down a lot. The footswitch was made out of pinball buttons. The buttons were from a pinball machine. I had four buttons to go forward, backward, left, and right. It was okay, but the buttons weren't reliable.

When I was an adult, I got my first power chair because I was getting ready to move into the group home. I still wasn't feeling like having a power chair because I didn't want my pushing leg to become weak. When I was out running errands such as shopping, boardwalks, going out to eat and traveling long distances, I brought my power chair. When I was back in the group home, I stayed in my manual wheelchair.

When my power chair went 'on the fritz,' I got mad. That happened a lot to me because my power chair had a mind of its own sometimes. When this happened, I couldn't control my power chair at all. The buttons got stuck when I pressed them, so I crashed into people or went around in circles. People thought I was doing it on purpose, but I wasn't!

For my second power chair, they found a circular toggle footswitch from England. My vendor bought the footswitch for me and it worked and lasted for years. I just stepped on the footswitch with my foot in the direction I wanted to go. The power chair went that direction and I had to hold my foot on the switch to keep it moving. I had to take my foot off the switch when I wanted to stop. That was perfect for me.

At this time, I was attending Brookdale. On my day off I practiced driving in my new power chair. My biggest challenge was going through doorways. There were buttons on the side of the doors to open the doors. I pushed the door buttons, but as soon as I was getting ready to go through the doors, they closed on me! I never was good at going through the doorways. I got smart: I waited for somebody else to open the doors!

All good things must come to the end. That is my favorite saying in this book, but that wasn't the end for the power chair for me. After I had my neck operation, I lost a lot of movement. I tell everybody that when you turn 45, it is downhill for them. In my case I went downhill very slowly. I remembered that my parents had told me not to get old. I laughed at them at the time, but as it turned out they were right.

I really thought my power chair days were over after my operation, but somehow, I got my determination back. I figured if I was sitting up and not in pain anymore then I had everything. I talked to my physical therapist about getting a new power chair because my leg wasn't working anymore. I told them to take my old power chair, because I didn't want it anymore. I knew that seeing my old power chair would be hard for me, not being in it.

My physical therapist decided to get me a chin switch to drive with my new power chair. Not the best thing for my neck, but it was better than nothing.

I decided on a purple power chair because I love purple. A few months passed, and my power chair came. I was so happy! Eventually, I went out in the community by myself again. I am still a little upset about my leg not working like it used to. Well, it's okay because at least I can say, yes, I used to push myself when I was younger!

Children with disabilities should do as much as possible when they are younger because you never know what the future holds for you. If children are capable of walking, they should be walking at whatever age they can. They should do as much as possible while they can still do those things for themselves. As they get older, they can say, "I walked by myself when I was younger." If they take time to write down their experiences, they will be able to share them with others later on, just as I am doing with all the wonderful things I wrote down throughout the years and now can pass on to everybody in my first book and now in this one.

Why me?

I think I may written this for an English course in Brookdale in the 1990's. I always had Determination. I wanted to live on my own and I did. Even though I loved my parents, I had to move on with my life!

# Why me; knowing what I want and achieving it to the best of my ability

## by Denise Ghizzone

Determination is knowing what you want and getting it done. You allow nothing to stand in your way. If you really want something, you feel nothing will stop your drive inside.

It is important knowing what I want in life and achieving it to the best of my ability. I have this drive within that makes me want to go after anything I want. If I set a goal, I strive to achieve it. It might not be how anybody else does it, but I will do it the best way I can. It might take me awhile to succeed, but I am a patient person. Time is on my side. Patience is a good thing to have. If I didn't have the good old "P" word, I wouldn't be the person who I am today.

Patience and determination are linked together. I am an over achiever because I go a step further. I like doing difficult things. It makes me think and answer things for myself.

The most significant thing I have achieved over the years is getting my apartment. That took determination and courage. About 9 years ago, the big event was moving out of my parents' house and into a group home. Although I have Cerebral Palsy and am wheelchair bound, I am active in all aspects of life; however, I need assistance with daily things, such as bathing, feeding, dressing, and other routines during the day. I knew my parents couldn't do everything for me the rest of their lives. It was time for me to be on my own.

Where I went during the day was called Ladacin Network. It is an agency which deals with physical challenges. One day, they talked about building group homes for Ladacin Network. They asked everybody if they would like to put their name on a list to live in a group home someday. I was 18 years of age, so I didn't have to get permission from my parents to put my name on the list.

I got home, I told my parents what I did, and they were concerned about it. Once they knew the whole deal, what a group home was and the details of living there, they were happy for me. Ladacin Network trained us to be more independent in daily living such as managing a check book, cooking, how to cope with things when they come up, etc.

My independence is very important to me. Being in a wheelchair is very difficult, but I have lots of determination. I am bright enough to know that I have to have a life beyond my family. My family knew I wasn't living with them forever. I was determined to get into my own place eventually. Being on a waiting list wasn't easy. I had to be evaluated and learn more things for myself. Being very patient was the key to my success.

My determination to move was hard because my family had done everything for me. Sometimes I went over my friend's house and she took care of me for a little while. I used to go to camp for the summers, but otherwise my family took care of me. It was nice. I figured something had to happen. I had to keep my mind focused on getting out on my own and starting to do things on my own.

Thinking positive helps, but I do have some days that I want to stay in bed and keep to myself.

Fortunately, I rarely feel like that. So many people who are like me think they are useless and keep to themselves. Being in a wheelchair is a fact of life, they have to deal with their situations. If they can't face reality, they are living in their own little world. That is very lonely place to be. I can't see myself being narrow minded like that.

Once I knew that Ladacin was building the group homes, I was so very happy. It took a while to get everything together to build them.

Meanwhile, Ladacin had classes on keeping a check book, planning meals, keeping house, and getting transportation out in the community. It took time, but I got it all under my belt. Now, I can't physically do all those things for myself. I also can't talk, so I have to use a computer or an alphabet board to direct my needs, the right way to lift me, taking me to the bathroom, cooking my meals, feeding me, and just taking care of me the way I want. If you try to lift me the wrong way, you might hurt me or yourself really bad.

About five years later, there were already two group homes built. One group home is in Lakewood and the other one is in Neptune. Ladacin had to pick six girls and six boys out of a group of 100 people from Monmouth and Ocean Counties.

It was a difficult choice to make because everybody had different reasons why they wanted to move. Some of the reasons were: they needed a place badly, they lived in a nursing home, their parents couldn't take care of them, or they needed socialization. They picked the twelve names, but I wasn't one of them.

I was disappointed and hurt. They told me I was a great candidate, but I wasn't a priority on the list. It was hard to hear, but I dealt with it. Then they told me they were going to build another one in Long Branch. It took about a year to build. As I waited for that group home to be built, I built up my confidence again and just went on living life.

Finally, the group home opened, and I was on the list to go. My family was happy for me. As for me, I was very excited because I was going to be out on my own. All that determination was worth my trouble. Being patient helped a lot.

I had to be more patient once I moved into the group home. For instance, Ladacin hired staff to assist us with our daily living tasks. Most of the people were willing to help us, but some of the people were difficult to get along with. It was their attitude mostly. They didn't like people telling them what to do. At first, it used to bother me. So many people take care of me, I don't care anymore. It isn't like me overall, but I can't deal with people who won't listen to me. Sometimes I will get somebody who's interested in Cerebral Palsy taking care of me for the week and I can direct them. Most of them tell me that I have a good outlook on life and a wonderful spirit. I don't know why I have a positive attitude, but I have to keep my peace of mind. I always think somebody is worse off than me. As long I have my mind going, I am great.

The group home had lots of opportunities for me, such as going out more, food shopping, having parties, and being myself. The group home had a certain level of supervision. I always had to go a step further beyond everybody else. Some people told me I should have my own apartment. I got used to the group home and I really liked it. But eventually I realized that living with five other people wasn't for me. I wanted some quiet and relaxation. In the group home, it was never quiet.

About 5 years later, Ladacin told us it was time to move. They built apartments in Lakewood and they moved some of us down there. They also had empty apartments in Neptune. I was asked to move there. Within me, I knew that wasn't what I wanted, but I was afraid of making a change out of group home living.

My determination and positive attitude got me to my own apartment. I was somewhat happy. The best part of moving into my own apartment was, I got to buy my own furniture and decorate my own apartment. The most important things I bought a bed and dresser. My parents bought me a bed. The headboard is made out of cherry wood and the wood smells brand new. It felt smooth in the grooves where the wood was cut. The mattress felt slippery and new against my body. The bed bounced when my body got in it. I bought a black, gray, pink, tan, white comforter, sham and curtains to match. The colors matched the rug because the rug was light brown with a tint of white mixed into it. I also got myself a dresser, I wanted a strong and fancy one. The dresser that I found was made out of shining, black lacquer with six long drawers in the front. Two small drawers on top have mirrors inside the bottom of both drawers. On eight drawers there is greenish color mixed into the shining, black dresser. I really enjoyed that very much.

Now that I have settled into that apartment, I am enjoying my privacy and peace a lot. I am enjoying my peace and my place because I like my independence. I like to do what I want to do.

Being determined and patient took me a long way. I have achieved a lot, living in my own apartment, going to Brookdale, and getting financial aid. Even just enjoying life is among the things I have achieved in my life already. I have to be active because if I am not, I feel like nothing. Achieving things is important to me.

## Personal Assistance Model

This is a speech I wrote for Ladacin Network new staff orientation, both for day programs and residence facilities. I have been at Ladacin almost all my life. I am an old pro at their mission. Today I give speeches such as this to new staff and similar speeches to the younger students to help them learn to communicate their needs to somebody who can help them.

This was written a long time ago, but people go by this philosophy at Ladacin to this day.

Thank you for coming today, I am going to talk about the Personal Assistance Model philosophy. I will explain to you why it is important for our programs and residences, and help you understand my concerns about why we should follow this model. Before residential services got started, the adult clients had never received personal care from any other people besides their own families or nurses. Receiving help from outside of that circle of people is difficult to do at first. I have been in Ladacin residential services since I was 22 years old.

Recently, I think the Personal Assistant Model philosophy got lost somewhere. It is not anybody's fault. Although little has changed in our needs over the years, people have different ideas about what personal assistance is. To me, that is sad because some of older clients were trained to direct you with our care. If we don't have the opportunity to direct our care, what is the sense of you being at Ladacin. At least this is how I feel.

The Personal Assistance Model was designed for clients of Cerebral Palsy to be independent. Before moving into housing, we have to learn how to direct other people in providing care to us. Most of us came from nursing homes and our parents' homes. We didn't have many opportunities to do anything for ourselves. We hardly made decisions or went out by ourselves. There are a lot of things that we can do, but we must have a little help during the day. Directing our care is very important to us. If we aren't given the opportunity, what is there to do? Maybe everybody doesn't want to direct their care the way I do. That is their choice.

Being disabled is a disadvantage of our lives, but we must make the best of it. It is hard living in a wheelchair, but we also have feelings like you. Some of us have problems dealing with that. It may not be anything to you, but it is a big deal to us. Nobody knows what it feels like being in a wheelchair unless you experience it. Most of our clients are born with a disability of some sort. This is a fact of life for us and we must live with it!

I want to take time to mention this: I appreciate that being a personal assistant is a hard job. Giving assistance to somebody else is not easy. Sometimes our personalities may clash. Dealing with people is hard. We each have our own disposition that affects the way we act and react to things. Everybody gets into their moods or forgets things. However, we clients depend on you staff for help with our care.

Most people are very nice and have great strengths. But sometimes we clients are not heard. Following our directions is the key to success for the Personal Assistance Model. You are our hands. If you don't do something the way we ask, then the Personal Assistance Model is not working.

Here is a bad example of being a personal assistant. One day I tried to tell my assistant to make my wheelchair seat belt tighter. They were rushing to get out of my apartment and I wasn't given any help. I gave up after a half hour of asking because they weren't getting it. This is my safety we are talking about. Plus, I can sit better when it is tight. I asked another assistant to help with my wheelchair seatbelt, it took two seconds to tighten. The first personal assistant made me mad. You need to take your time and listen to our directions such as the second person did. That is how the model works. It will be less stressful for all of us. I know it may be faster your way, but that is not how the Personal Assistance Model works.

I am going to give some more examples of situations that have happened to me. Being in a wheelchair all day, I need to be comfortable and look nice. I go out in public and people notice my appearance. I want to look great because you never know, I may find somebody that I like, ha ha ha. We represent the agency and housing. A poor appearance can fall back on the wrong person. Another staff person or a stranger may ask us what happened, and it reflects back on the quality of your care standards. One of my biggest things for me is that my clothes must be to put on right so that nothing is falling off me during the day. For example, my sneakers need to be tight. What if they come off somewhere and nobody is around? It could happen, you don't know. I think people think that I am just being a pain, but I am not. I know from experience what could happen during the day. There was the time I used to push myself in my manual wheelchair and it was a fact, I couldn't push myself without my sneakers. I think of these things before they happen.

I have another example. I like my power wheelchair foot straps to be very tight. It helps me to drive and sit better in my wheelchair. What if my foot came out of my straps on my power wheelchair? If my straps aren't tight, I may not have help until I get home. I would be uncomfortable all day and that is not a good feeling. All I am saying is that you don't know what is going to happen to us out in public. We want to be comfortable and look presentable. Whether you are in a wheelchair or not, I know you would want to look nice when you go out. I know this may sound ridiculous to you, but it really isn't.

Just imagine you are in a wheelchair and you must depend on others to help you go to the bathroom. You really need to go, so you ask somebody to take you. They say go to your room and they'll come soon. You wait for fifteen minutes and think you are being very patient. You call down for them again. Now they come. How do they know you can wait fifteen minutes? Sometimes when we must go, we must go. When we drink, we must go to the bathroom, that is a fact of life. Nobody can pick what time they must go to the bathroom. We need liquid to survive. I don't want to go to the bathroom more, but I have to drink more to be healthy. I can't win either way.

Also, when you are putting away something of ours, please let us know where you put it. Otherwise we may not be able to find it. I lost my identification once because somebody put it in the wrong spot of my wallet by mistake. Luckily my friend found it. It was in my wallet all the time. I was mad because I asked two personal assistants to find my identification, but they couldn't. I know nobody is perfect.

It is not funny, but many people seem to leave gloves in our rooms. When we ask a staff person to take the gloves, we are often told those gloves are not theirs. It can be comical living here. I think what everybody needs to work on, is taking their time and not rushing around. Please listen to us. This is our home and our lives. You are here to assist us in doing things. We are all unique individuals and would like to enjoy life the best we can. Life is too short to rush. I hope you understand that I am trying to help and not criticize. I am grateful to all of you for working in this residence. Thank you.

I created that speech several years back but Ladacin goes by these principles to this day. Some people get this concept faster than other people. Very few completely fail to get the concept. It is tough to train people who have never worked for people with disability before. So many years have passed and there are so many different clients at Ladacin now. They can each make their own decisions, but in many cases, it is very hard for them to communicate to others. Your patience and willingness to listen will go a long way towards enabling that communication.

Even though some of us can't do certain things, we have a lot of talented clients here. Just to name a few, we have artists that paint with their mouth, singers, dancers, sewers, public speakers, writers, guitar players, and many others.

People with disabilities have a lot of talents just as other people do. Even though they are sitting in a wheelchair, you can never know what talent they have or what they can do for themselves unless you ask.

## Art

A lot of people take for granted writing their name or painting pictures. People with disabilities wish that writing or painting came that easy for them. For some it doesn't. When I was little, I could write and paint with my hand or head pointer.

In 1983, the Schroth school hired an art teacher named Melody Lane Smith. She was an outgoing person. Melody taught me to paint some wonderful paintings. She taped a paint brush to my head pointer. She would put different color of paints and water in cups and tape everything down in front of me including the canvas. That was how I painted wonderful paintings. I created beach scenes, park scenes, and still life. She taught me how to make shadows in my paintings. I really enjoyed creating different scenes.

Most people have no idea what it is like signing an X for your name on important documents. An X isn't personal, and an X isn't your own name. I was determined to have my own personal signature!

The reason why I wanted my very own signature was because writing an X for my name wasn't personal. As the same as I painted with my head pointer on that was how I used to write my name at that time. Melody taped a pencil to my head pointer, I could write my name. I wanted to write my name smaller because it was very large and didn't fit on the line when I needed to sign my name on something. I asked Melody if there was a way she could teach me to write my name smaller and legible for others to understand. She worked with me for years. Let me tell you, I had that poor woman going crazy, but in the end, I got my personal signature!

It took seven years just to finish this long drawn out project. I thought it would be a simple project but take it from me, it wasn't! You don't want to hear what I put Melody through trying to figure how I could get my own personalized signature!

Finally, several years later she found something in a catalog that she ordered supplies from. It was a stamper where you could create your own stamper. She thought of me right away. She showed it to me, but there was a small problem. Whatever you wanted to create, it had to be small enough to put on a stamp.

We decided to make my name small. There I was again, writing my name for the millionth time. I picked a couple from the best I could write to choose from. Then we picked my best one somehow. We both recognized that I can't write my name twice without having it turn out different. My best one overall turned out too big and too light! She took a thin, white piece of paper and traced my name with a dark pencil.

Next, Melody shrunk my name on a copier machine. She kept shrinking it until it was only three inches. Finally, after five tries she got my name down to size. I wrote a check for the stamper and mailed it off.

We were waiting patiently for my personalized signature stamper. Eight weeks later it came; I think she was more excited than I was! Who could blame her because she had been working on it for the last seven years. I was amazed at how they could put my name in a stamper. I just loved it! When it came, I stamped my name all over the place on important documents.

Now that I am older, I appreciate my personalized signature stamper because nobody needs to help me by putting a pencil in my hand so I can write my X on important documents. Nobody on this earth has my hand writing!

My head pointer days are over, but I still have some of my paintings and of course my personalized stamper. I don't leave home without it!

All my thanks go to Melody Lane Smith for not giving up on our project of creating my own signature stamper. For me, it is more than an object. It represents the care and respect she showed me in enabling me to sign documents. Everyone needs help in different ways, and we never know how we can enhance someone else's life just by offering practical help!

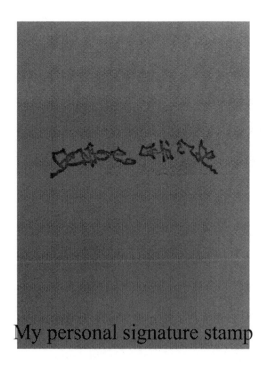

My personal signature stamp

## Life experiences!

I thought a personal love life was out of the question for me. I have always talked to people of the opposite sex. In our society many people feel disabled people can't share feelings with a nondisabled person. I believe that sometimes people can't help falling for certain people. Everybody has the right to love or to be loved by anybody they want. It doesn't matter if they are in a wheelchair or can't communicate. People can love and express themselves in other ways. Nondisabled people often feel that people with disabilities can't handle relationships. I disagree with that. Having relationships is a part of life. Whoever they choose to love, the other person has a special place in their heart.

The relationships I have had with men have been just friendships. That was as far as the relationship went. Yes, my thoughts overpowered me with some nice things when I was in my teens and early twenties. I was hoping some of my thoughts would come true.

Some things change when you least expected. I liked men and/or men liked me. I wanted to see where it might lead. I will tell you brief flashbacks about those relationships from a long time ago. Those relationships are done and over. Did I regret having them? No, but if I had a chance I would like to do some things over again. What was the biggest problem having relationships? When you are living under somebody else's roof and having 24 hours care, then you don't have the privacy required for a relationship with a man. People wanted to know everything about the people who came to see me throughout the years. That was my biggest problem! People with disabilities have an ongoing lack of privacy. It is difficult to build a relationship with a man when you are always around other people where you live. Would I have chosen the same men to have a relationship with? Yes, definitely I would, because I really liked them. They were my knights in shiny armors!

*First flashback*:

Thinking back on my teenage years, I have to admit I was a big flirt. I was 'boy crazy.' Every boy or man I saw, I flirted with them. My best friend Karen has two brothers. When I met them, a big smile came on my face. I thought they were cute and every time I saw them I flirted with them. They would flirt back.

Once there was a man, I used to flirt with him all of a time. I talked to him with my communication board and he was very nice. I had a crush on him. Being a teenager, I used to day dream about him. There was nothing wrong with day dreaming!

*Second flashback*:

I preferred and dated these disabled walking men. The one man I knew for a long time. I used to like him when we were kids. When I was younger, we were together only once a year. In between, I missed those times with him. When we got older, he used to come to see me more often. Sometimes we hung out together. We went out to lunch and had some drinks.

*Third flashback*:

Somebody was in my life for nine years. I never thought I would have a relationship with him because I saw him as a friend.

I asked myself why was this abled body man saying lovely things to me like he would say to his girlfriend? I never thought he was coming on to me and I didn't want him to stop. Of course, it was nice getting that kind of attention from a man. Once he told me how he felt. I was shocked! I told myself this wasn't happening to me. A couple of times we were alone together and that was very special to me.

At different times, I had two different men who liked me and talked to me like a normal woman. Being disabled, you have to go for something and take a chance. I am a good judge of who I can trust.

Looking back on those moments, I treasure them. Those relationships didn't last too long. Unfortunately, I don't see those men anymore, but I still talk to them sometimes. I think of them often. They broke my heart. Everybody gets their hearts broken, whether they are disabled or not.

I hope those men know and remember how special they were to me. I miss those men to this day. I never thought I could have a relationship, but I have had multiple friendships. My point is people with disabilities can have relationships with anybody they want. As for me, I wasn't successful, but I had nice experiences trying. I appreciated those men spending time with me. I don't want to say who those men are because I still value their friendships.

## I finally became an Author!

Ever since I can remember I have loved to write my thoughts down on paper for people to understand what I am thinking. When I was a child and teenager, I used to write letters to my family and friends on my typewriter. My mom used to mail them out for me. Since I have a creative mind I wrote my childhood memories on paper. When computers came out at Ladacin they taught me how to work them. After that my dad bought a new computer for me a couple times throughout the years; each time with a printer.

I am going out date myself when I say this: I had an Apple computer with a floppy diskette, so I could save my writings. Next, I had a computer with a hard disk. Eventually, flash drives were available on all computers, so I managed to keep all my writings. I have big binders full of my life events throughout the years, as well as short stories I wrote for my creative writing classes at Brookdale Community College. They are still here to this day! Once I rewrote one story on my computer from paper. The story was so old that the ink had faded a little. I just had to laugh to myself.

For years, I tried to submit my stories to various magazines and some publishers online. I wasn't successful. I got a lot of rejection letters. One story got on the internet on somebody's website, and that was pretty cool. The magazines had too many rules. Once I took a journalism class and I failed it. Journalism wasn't for me because there were too many rules to follow. I love creative writing because I can write what I want. For years, I was asking people to help me to publish my life story, but I got no takers. Even I asked my old teacher Mr. Brady! But he is retired, and he turned me down. He corrected a lot of it for me. I told him he could be famous with me and he still wasn't interested! I even asked my therapists to help me, but no takers!

I asked somebody else to help and this came together perfectly for me. One of my bosses from Ladacin found out and she asked me what was I trying to do? I told her I was trying to write my life story. I had written these incredible stories throughout my life and I wanted to write a book. I told her I had asked around, but I didn't get very far. She told me she would see what she could do. She got in touch with somebody who helped a mutual friend with her book. She set up a meeting.

I said to myself, I finally did it, I'm going to be an Author! When my boss told me what was the day of the meeting with the editor, I went home and started preparing what I wanted to say to him in my communication device.

The meeting day came, and I learned that his name is John Feaver. Using my communication device, I explained to him what I wanted to accomplish. I suggested to him I would email him my chapters, because that would be the fastest way I could do it. When he said he would help me as I sat there in all of my glory, a huge smile came on my face. I liked him, and I was determined to get this accomplished once for all. He said, you can email your chapters. I told him that was okay. I was thinking in the back of my mind that he's going to help me after I had waited so long. I'm going to be an Author finally! And to think that people had said I should stop writing.

I went home and kept emailing him my chapters. I think I made his computer run all night! It took a few months to do it. I would send drafts, and he would email back a version with edits and comments or questions. With my creative mind and his editing skills we got it done successfully!

A few months later, John asked me what picture I wanted on the cover of my book. I had a perfect picture, my Brookdale graduation picture! I was sitting up nice and tall with a pretty smile on my face. It was perfect for my book. I thought my mom would have loved that. I dedicated my book to my loving mom!

John and I were brainstorming on a name for my book. We decided on the title: Determination, What I'm all about by Denise Ghizzone! His daughter designed my cover. When I saw what she had designed, I was awed by the cover!

My goal was going to come true! Years of my dedication from my writings and education from typewriter to different computers, I successfully was doing what I wanted all of my life: becoming an Author!

John found a website that printed books. A couple of days later, my book came in. It was perfect, and I told everybody I was an Author! John set it up on Amazon for me. I told everybody I knew that my book was on Amazon and to please buy one. Two years it's still selling!

Mr. Brady bought a few for his family and friends. He even came over to get my autograph. Anyhow, Mr. Brady got my autograph on the books that he had bought.

My determination got me to be an Author. It took me a long time, but I successfully achieved my goal. Now you are reading my second book, I am excited being an Author! People with disabilities can be successful like anybody in this world. They need some help along the way. There are no limitations with me; I can do anything in people's eyes!

Throughout this (my second) book I have told you about the things that I have accomplished and about people's attitudes towards people with disabilities and me in particular. It really does matter what you call people with disabilities. Nobody likes to be called names or made fun of. We are still human beings just like you. We can love, talk, and sometimes have even achieved the impossible. We might have to take our time and get some help along the way. Doesn't everybody need some help over their lifetime? Everybody likes to have some respect, have others talk with you rather them having you talk at them like a thing. Respect goes a long way. You never know what you could find in somebody in a power chair. They could be a teacher, an author, or both such as me.

## Creative writing

I wrote this story in my first creative writing course. when I attended Brookdale. Now I am 51 years old. Most of these things haven't happened to me, but I do have a job. I have no boyfriend or husband. I love creative writing, it puts me a different place and I can be anything I want to be.

The assignment was, where will you be when you are 40?! At the time of writing I was in my 20's and my imagination was filled with different ideas I had locked up in my head. These next few stories will show that nothing is wrong with imagination! I hope you will enjoy them like I enjoyed creating them.

# When I am 40 years old

When I become 40 years old I will be very happy. I will have graduated college in 1993 and my major will have been Data processing. After graduating, I will have written my resume and sent some to all different companies in New Jersey. Having lived in a group home in Neptune for 6 years, I didn't want to move out of there. Nevertheless, a month later I got a call from AT&T and my assistant got me on the telephone with my communication device (the person who was calling me knew from my resume that I had a communication device). They wanted me to come down for an interview that Monday at 10:00 A.M. Excited, I arranged for somebody to take me.

When Monday came, I met the person who had called me. Her name was Mrs. Brown and she was very nice. She interviewed me, and I told her what my needs were. She told me that I could start working as soon as I could find somebody to help me with my needs.

It took me about a month to learn the ropes. Then I met a lot new friends and sometimes after work we went out and had a couple of drinks.

A year later a man came into my life. He worked at AT&T. His name was Tom Hudson and he was 5'4" tall.

He had short black hair and his eyes were blue. He was really built because he used to live in Florida and work out in a fitness place. I taught him the ropes about the job. After a while we started going out for dinner, dancing, and hanging together. We loved each other very much. He took me to meet his parents and I took him to meet mine. We dated for three years.

One spring night, he took me out to a romantic restaurant up north. After dinner we went dancing. Tom ordered us some drinks. He went down on one knee and reached into his pocket. He took out an engagement ring and slipped it on my finger; then he proposed to me. Yes, I will, I said. Then I cried and gave him a big hug. It was the happiest night of my life. We decided to get married in November. We went to tell Tom's parents. His mother took one look at our faces and screamed out with happiness for us. His father was happy for us, too.

The next day we told my parents, and they were thrilled too. We also told our friends in the group home. A month later, they threw Tom and me a little bridal shower. Tom and I started to look for a little house to buy. Finally, we found a house in Holmdel. About a month later, Tom called around for a homemaker to live with us. He found a person called Beth with two children in college. She used to be a personal assistant in a group home in Dallas, Texas. She moved to New Jersey five years ago because her husband died in a car accident. Understandably, she wanted to go far away from Texas. I started moving out of the group home two months later. Tom and I got married and it was a big wedding. All our friends were there. The wedding was in Tom's parents' house. Everything went great.

For our honeymoon we went on a cruise to Florida to Disney World for three weeks and then to Virginia for two weeks. We had the best time together.

Finally, it was time to go back home. My life changed for the better. Now I have a husband to share things with. I also have a house of my own.

Nine years have passed, and Tom and I are happier than ever now. I quit my job because I started my own business at home. I am a tutor and people come to my house to learn about computers. Tom sometimes helps me with tutoring.

P.S. I hope this story really comes true!

*This was from my first creative writing class.*

## A day out in the country

My friend Anthony and I made plans to spend the day together. We went to a park for the day. We drove way out in the country. It was a pretty spring day. I was looking out the window, while Anthony was coasting down the road. All of the trees were blooming, and the grass had turned green again. Finally, we got to the park and all the birds were singing. In the park, there was a garden filled with all kinds of flowers. We walked through the garden. The garden was filled with different kind of colors like bright red for roses, light purple for violets, and yellow for tulips. We found a bench under a big old tree, and we sat and talked for a while.

It started to rain a little. Anthony and I sat watching the raindrops falling and it was so peaceful that we didn't want to leave. I really liked the smell of the rain. Everything smells so fresh in the spring after it rains. The rain stopped, and the sun shone more brightly than ever. All of the birds came out to sing again. The grass was greener, and everything was brighter.

It was getting late and we were hungry, too. So, we went to a hamburger place to eat. We ordered two cheeseburgers, some french fries, and two vanilla milkshakes. We were still hungry, so we shared a big banana split together. We ordered everything on it. We didn't finish the whole thing between the two of us. Then we paid our bill and headed home.

*These are more of my creative writings ...*

# My favorite food

I like different foods, and it is really hard to pick one. If I have to choose, I say it is pizza! I will describe why I like pizza, how it smells, what it looks like and the way people feed it to me.

I am part Italian, and I enjoy eating Italian foods. I think pasta is the best out of everything in this world. My mom grew her own tomatoes in the summer in our backyard. She took care of her little garden. She weeded and watered throughout the summer. During the winter, she made Italian dishes all of the time, such as stuffed shells, baked ziti, macaroni, spaghetti, meatballs, and of course her famous eggplant parmesan. The end of the summer she made her own tomato sauce for the winter. I like the smell of Italian foods cooking in our kitchen. Once in a while, she made Italian chicken legs. To make Italian chicken legs, mix eggs, add granted cheese, and roll the chicken in those ingredients. Then roll the chicken in bread crumbs and fry them in olive oil. I can eat five of them at once.

Once my brother made pizza from scratch while I watched. He put on the pizza my mom's homemade sauce, grated cheese, mozzarella cheese, pepperoni, sausages, oil, oregano, and olive oil. I like all that stuff on my pizza. I tried his pizza when it was done, and it was great.

Pizza smells terrific when it comes out of the oven. It has such an Italian smell to it. When you take it out of the oven, it bubbles on top. Also, when you cut the pizza, the mozzarella cheese sticks to the knife. The way pizza looks, it makes you want to take a bite out of it right away without letting it cool. It has a very interesting coloring to the food. There are different colors in pizza, such as brown, green, white, and of course red. If you buy your pizza, often the crust is chewy and hard. I like my crust soft and chewy, so I prefer when it's home-cooked.

I need to be fed, and whoever is feeding me pizza will get messy! I like to bite my pizza and the feeder gets mad at the pizza because the sauce and the mozzarella cheese gets all over the place. I also sometimes bite their fingers, and they get mad at me. I can't help it because they put their fingers too close to my mouth. I can see it happening if somebody new is feeding me, but when somebody knows me for a long time, they should know better. People that are new to me tend to cut my pizza into little pieces and then feed me with a fork. I really hate when people do that to me. That is taking the easy way out. I am sorry but that just isn't the way Italians eat their pizza. Pizza is supposed to get all over you when you eat it. I think pizza is the most fun food to eat in the world. I don't think that I know a person who doesn't like pizza. Pizza is nutritious for you. Pizza is also fun to have somebody feed me, but very messy.

# My adventure as a bear

One fall night, I slept over my friend's house. She lived in the country near a forest. The forest had a lot of old big trees and caves. It was very dark all the time and nobody went near it because there were wild animals. There were wild birds, deer, snakes, and bears, and who knows what else. My friend and I slept outside in her backyard with sleeping bags.

I woke up and realized that a strange thing had happened to me. Somehow, I was in the forest. I looked around, but there was no way out. No matter where I looked there were big old trees and dirt on the ground. I heard all kind of sounds like wild birds fighting, bears growling, deer footprints crackling on the dry leaves. When I tried to scream, I made this big growl; what came out was a sound that you never want to hear in your life. I felt and looked at myself. I had turned into a bear! I had brown soft brown fur and big brown eyes. I also had big sharp teeth. I was 7 feet tall and very fat too.

When I walked, everything started to shake. I walked around for a long time. I finally found a stream. I tried to fit into the stream, but I was too fat and tall. I got down on all fours, put my head down, and started to drink the water.

After that, I looked for something to eat. I found a bees' nest in a tree and stuck my paw in it (I was glad that there weren't any bees in the nest!) and came out with some honey. It was good.

I followed the sound of bears' growls, thinking maybe they would lead me to their cave. I followed the growls for a long time and found one cave. But there wasn't one bear anywhere to be found. The cave was pitch black. I went to my sleeping bag and lay on top of it. I fell asleep. When I woke up, I was back to myself. It was all a dream!

# When I was a Barbie doll

One summer night, I was tired and went to bed early. When I woke up I realized I was a Barbie doll. My body was made of plastic. I was 10 inches high and only my head, arms, and legs could move. I had little blue eyes which were made out of paper and stayed open all of the time. I had shiny, blonde, long hair.

I was in my dream house. I walked through the whole house. I walked upstairs to my pink bedroom. I was looking through some clothes in my dresser. I found a red dress and under my bed there were high heels. So, I put the dress and high heels on. On top of my dresser. I found a little red ribbon for my hair.

I looked out my bedroom window; in front of my house there was my hot pink sport car. I went downstairs and got my car keys on my kitchen table. I went out of the house. It was a nice hot night for a drive. I got into my car and went driving around. I drove fast like lightning. I went out looking for Ken. I finally found Ken coming out from a bar. So, I beeped my horn at him, he jumped into my car, and off we went.

We drove for hours, finally we ended at some beach. We decided to go on the beach. I opened my trunk of my car and took out a bright yellow blanket. Ken took his shoes off and I took my high heels off too. We left them in my car. Ken and I took a walk on the beach and talked for a while. It was very quiet except for the waves coming in and out. We found a spot to spread our blanket for us to lay on. We got comfortable on the blanket.

Before we knew it, it was morning. We went back to my car and I dropped Ken off at his house. I went to bed when I got home.

Made in the USA
Middletown, DE
21 March 2019